Burning Coal

Sara Khalid

BookLeaf Publishing
India | USA | UK

Burning Coal © 2024 Sara Khalid

All rights reserved.

No part of this publication may be reproduced, stored in a retrieval system, or transmitted, in any form or by any means, electronic, mechanical, photocopying, recording or otherwise, without the prior written permission of the presenters.

Sara Khalid asserts the moral right to be identified as author of this work.

Presentation by *BookLeaf Publishing*

Web: www.bookleafpub.com

E-mail: info@bookleafpub.com

ISBN: 9789358315363

First edition 2024

This is dedicated to my parents, sisters and husband.

2023

Everywhere is colour, swimming, olive trees and joy.
There is an endless meadow where you see a girl and a boy.
They are playing in the grass with delicate flower crowns on their heads.
An infinity horizon, fruit jewels on trees- "I love it here" the girl said.
They return to their modestly beautiful home to the welcome of their mother's smile.
Her eyes are oceans of kindness, she is a vault to the upcoming trial.
She holds secrets in her heart of what has happened in years gone by.
Her mission is to cultivate happiness, never let her children cry.
This becomes harder as the birds turn to rockets in the sky.
The grass is turning to rubble and the boy and girl begin to ask why.
They are told they need to leave, that this is no longer their home.
The mother reassures them that this is a mistake, they will be left in peace alone.

Bedtime stories turn into constant repetitive prayers.
The fire outside is never ending and the girl, becoming anxious, starts to pull out her own hair.
The shining armour of their mother begins to slowly crack.
She sheds silent tears, the children overhear that the hospital is under attack.
The hospital where their uncle works, fixing both hearts and bones with a constant smile.
They used to love hearing about his operations, to think of it he had not visited in a while.
The boy is defiant and determined, he wants to go to school.
There he had friends, he played football in a Ronaldo shirt, he was cool.
He escapes one day, determined to make it to class.
There are loud noises, then everything is silent, his body is covered in glass.
His ears are ringing, his hands are shaking, he is only eight years old.
But he knows his way back home and begins to run towards it down the now destroyed road.
On arrival there is nothing, everything has gone.
He sees his mother sobbing- "Everything is done."

He forces himself to look and there is the girl in his mother's lap.
She is dead, he drops to his knees, everything goes black.
The boy's grief is on fire he doesn't understand why.
They now pray six times a day, and all his mother does is cry.
He is only eight years old but life has forced him to become grown.
He is disgusted by the lies sold as truth, he will never leave a place that his own.
His anger overflows when the newsreaders say everything is made up.
He feels he is losing his mind, the girl was real, she was a person. It was getting too much.
The girl had big dreams, she wanted to go to university and design toys.
He vows to never let anyone forget her, or the colour, swimming, olive trees and joy.

Safety

My mother lifts up her right index finger,
holding it there a few seconds.
A small while later she turns her head right and
then left.
I lay my tired head in her lap, as she brings up
both hands in prayer.
Her dupatta smells of home. Her bangles sound
like peace.
All the hurricanes and tsunamis in my mind
stop.
Here, I am safe.

I want to move

I want to get on a plane and move to Pakistan.
I want to exist in colour, I want to hear the
Adhaan.
I want to live with my grandmother and she
could oil my hair.
I want to be greeted at the airport with that big
hit of hot air.
I want to drink fresh mango juice three times
every day.
I want to wear tailor made clothes that I've
helped craft and create.
I want to live in a house where my extended
family all live.
I want to be surrounded with stories, who did
you love, hate, forgive?
I'm told it's not that beautiful, I'm looking
through rose-tinted glass.
Your future and success depend on your name
and on your class.
The cost of living is sky high and people can't
afford to eat.
You have to bribe to get your job done, be wary
of everyone you meet.
So maybe I'm delusional, a UK born and bred.

But I feel my heart is pulling me towards my heritage.
I want to get on a plane and move to Karachi.
It might not be what I'm dreaming of, but I think there I'll feel more like me.

In me

If you see any resilience in me,
Pray for my Mother
Who taught me tawakkul and spreads glitter of positivity everywhere she goes.
If you see any humility in me,
Pray for my Father
Who taught me it's what you can do for others, known for being special by everyone he meets.
If you see any happiness in me,
Pray for my Sisters
Who surely will be the reason for my full heart and smile on my face.
If you see any calmness in me,
Pray for my Husband
Who pacifies the storm in my mind daily without ever getting tired.
If you see any love in me,
Pray for my Grandparents
Who lived a real life love story for us to aim towards.
If you see any enthusiasm in me,
Pray for my Teachers
The ones who believed in me and told me to carry on,
If you see any softness in me,

Pray for my Patients
The tears I've shared with their relatives, the tough decisions we've had to make together.
If you see any goodness in me,
Pray for my Parents and my Molvi Sahib
I wrote my first poem for them
And may the angel on their right shoulder never stop writing.

People doing things

I just love watching people doing things
Going to Leicester Square where the busker sings
A group of girls arrive and begin to dance
A confident boy pulls his girlfriend in "No, I can't, I can't!"
But he persuades her, and they begin to dance too
A crowd gathers together all singing the tune
The tired office workers after finishing their shift
See the opportunity for fun and start pumping their fists
A doctor in scrubs going to work through the night
Joins to sing the chorus surrounded by iPhone lights
For those few minutes of singing and dancing to Coldplay
Nothing else matters, everyone forgets it's a been tough day
Watching strangers who spent the day just trying to survive
Joined together in living, makes me feel alive

Oranges

I told my father I liked the orange that was in the fruit bowl.
The next day he brought me a whole crate.
He would bring me the tree if he could,
Or plant seeds of orange trees in the garden so I would have my own orange farm at my disposal.
Me and my sisters would take photos there and eat oranges till we were sick.
I would then move onto something else and he would do the same,
Listening carefully to what I liked, bringing crates of it the following day.

Mr and Mrs

You and me were in the centre of the room stood back to back,
Playing that game Mr and Mrs, everyone sat around poised to attack.
I thought we were surrounded with friends, if not friends then maybe colleagues,
Not sure what their game was, what they were hoping to achieve.
We didn't realise we were in a cage, and the cage was encircled with snakes,
We were about to be sadistic entertainment, stood there as bait.
The questions begun and they were wild beyond belief,
"Whose dad owns a corner shop?" "Whose brother drives taxis?"
"Who knows more Mohammeds?" "Who is a better Muslim?" "Who smells more of curry?"
My mouth was laughing, my eyes were empty and my knees trembled with worry.
I turned back to look into your Arab eyes,
You were uncomfortable too, we both wanted to cry.
But we were silent, we said nothing, continued to play and look down.

One confused snake justified "It's okay I can say this, I am also brown".
I don't know if you even remember this episode, how it made you feel,
We haven't spoken since then, but to me it was real.
Maybe I should have spoken up, made it stop, said these are not funny jokes,
But then again, it is not on me to have the conscious, why couldn't the snakes have spoke?
People now ask me why do you have very few friends from university,
"Choose loneliness over ill friends" – Imam Ali (A.S)

A COVID Haiku

Never-ending deaths
Parties in Westminister
We cannot forget

Deep Feeling

An elderly man sat a restaurant eating his meal alone
An international student asking the supermarket employee how microwave meals work
A young waiter who accidentally drops soup on a fancy diner
A little girl who runs to her mum after school to show her what she has drawn
A group of friends who throw their mortarboards high in the sky in achievement
A trio of friends where one is walking behind, attempting to get into conversation
A man who smiles knowingly when his girlfriend catches the bouquet of flowers thrown by the bride
A mother's silence who's daughter makes her sit alone instead of with her friends
A father's look when his son is no longer interested in spending time with him
A little boy's ecstasy when his older sister buys him a big balloon
A new doctor to the country, happily ignorant to the snide comments people make of his broken English

A shard of sunshine cutting through clouds on a gloomy day

The ordinary

Waking up in fresh white sheets
Turning the small lights on
A warm cup of tea where you can see the steam
White toast with melted butter and strawberry jam
Putting a jumper on that's been on the radiator
The smell of freshly washed clothes
Singing to the Jonas Brothers in the car
Chatting over lunch break about weekend plans
Hearing a patient's husband gush about his wife
The canteen serving my favourite meal
The rain stopping, the sun shining and a rainbow emerging
Catching up on Facetime with my family
An evening walk to get a hot chocolate
The joy in the ordinary

Sisterhood

If my life was made into a film for the big cinema screens,
What genre would it fit into, what would the story mean?
I would cast an up-and-coming Muslim actress who would play me,
Then the two most beautiful girls as my sisters, to complete the three.
The story would follow us three sisters and the audience would see,
How my life was saved by these two, daily and repeatedly.
The events would show although they're both younger, they look after me,
The middle acting as the eldest, the youngest providing the comedy.
You would see the youngest running around, cracking jokes, making everyone tea,
Whilst the middle stopped my panic attacks calmly saying "You have to listen to me."
Our kitchen discos, games nights and late nights baking sugar cookies,
The director would parallel with serious discussions about jobs and university.

The critics would write "a tale of sisterhood and soulmates, you must go and see!"
Thank you to my sisters, Alhamdullilah, you make my life a movie.

Half of my deen

He is a welcome cool breeze of air on a sweltering hot summers day,
He is reassurance, it's okay it's okay it's okay.
He is a blockbuster movie that you can't wait to go and see,
He is trust and stability, "Sara you can tell me."
He is a new book you want to spend all your time with,
He is generosity, you don't need to ask and he's ready to give.
He is a new handbag that you want to show off but also keep safe,
He is charisma, makes friends in every new place.
He is the first sip of water to break a long fast,
He is consideration, knows it's sin to break a heart.
He is a watch you've worked hard for, and so you're proud to wear
He is integrity, protects your name when you're not there.
He is the building that survives a catastrophic earthquake,
He is total honesty, finds it impossible to be fake.

He is a King and strives hard to treat me as Queen,
Alhamdullilah for him for completing half my deen.

That feeling

That
Finished my prayers,
Head still in sajdah,
Lying on the mat,
Crying my eyes out,
Gasping for air,
Seeking help desperately,
Feeling

I would walk

My sisters and me are sat on the floor of the family room,
The cricket is on, we're all watching together with a collective sense of doom.
England are scoring far too many runs,
Watching Pakistan flounder has never been fun.
Then the boys in green pick up and wickets start to fall,
One of the fast bowlers is close to a haul.
The next English batsman comes for his turn and is stood at the crease,
The crowd are so loud, all on their feet.
The ball swings in and he's obviously out,
The crowd are all up, there's 0 doubt.
The batsman doesn't move, he stays still,
The stadium is quiet waiting for the third umpire's will.
Supporters shaking their heads, a sea of disapproving green,
"We've seen this before, Trent Bridge 2013."
OUT- is the verdict on the big screen,
Me and my sisters let out a scream.
We turn to my father to ask him,
What would you have done if you were trying to win?

Quietly but firmly he says "I would walk."
Small in volume but profound, is how my Dad talks.
Those three words sum up who he is,
Integrity, honesty, loyalty- our family's king.

This is the thing

The thing they hate about you
The thing they tease you for
The thing they say you need help for
The thing they backbite about you
The thing they call you names about
The thing they make you feel insecure about
The thing they make you overthink about
The thing they make you feel small about
The thing they make you feel crazy about
Well, this is the thing.
The thing is something they wish they had
The thing is something they don't see in themselves
The thing is why someone will fall in love with you
The thing is a fair enough thing
The thing is something you've had to learn
The thing is a quality turned into an insult
The thing is criticised in guilt
The thing is what your family love you for
The thing the thing the thing.

Anxiety

Someone asked me what anxiety feels like
It's hard to put it into words
I guess if I had to it would be waves crashing in your stomach
It would be a multi-storey building sitting on your lungs
It would be your heart always running a race
It would be your mind stuck in a never ending maze
It would be an electric current constantly surging through your nerves
It would be your worst case scenario all the time
It would be over complicating the simplest of tasks
It would be an alarm clock waking you up hourly through the night
It would be looking up at the sky to find an ounce of peace from somewhere
It would be all of this, all at once, all the time
That's what anxiety feels like.

A day in the life

You wake up in the morning after a night when you have not had much sleep.
Sleep is for the lucky 9-5ers you think as you sit down to start the day of work.
Work is hard to do with no equipment and you are surrounded by beeps.
Beeps from the machines are something you have to learn to tune out but also keep an ear out in case they indicate danger.
Danger is hearing that a junior doctor is in critical care after crashing their car following a set of nights.
Nights, is what you're due to be working next week, the week before your exams.
Exams that you have to pay for yourself and are compulsory for you to progress but you have to study for whilst working full time.
Time never seems to be on your side, you come home from work just so you can revise.
Revise a few hours but your brain is fog because you haven't been able to switch off or go to the gym.
"Gym- £50" comes out of your account every month, yet you never go as it erodes out your already low pay.

Pay is something everyone thinks you have an abundance of but it's not true and you find it insulting and unfair.

Unfair is what your non medics friends say when you "don't know yet" if you can attend their wedding.

Wedding, "yes I understand you are getting married but you will still have to swap out of your on call."

Calls to your loved one complaining becomes the norm and you worry that you are beginning to change

Change is essential, change is necessary, change so we can do what we love without fear.

Sick

Sometimes I feel sick at the human race,
How many people have more than one face.
The way people forget the privilege they were born in,
This educated belief that there is no sin.
The modern way is to always put self first,
Pretending to be blind to those complaining of thirst.
The materialistic philosophy to always want more,
Young children demanding money to complete household chores.
The feeling of never meeting satisfaction,
Falling for corporate tricks of massive over consumption.
Social media tricking us that we're always worse off,
That for us in our warm lit houses, life is really tough.
Then, on other the side of the world, we see,
Children with nothing, out of rubble making beauty.
Mothers making beautiful childhoods despite having just one bed for seven,

And now it makes sense that the poor will make the majority of heaven.

The best of days

It is the middle of August in beautiful Pakistan,
The sun has set, creating a warm hazy calm.
The birds are singing and you can hear the children outside play,
The Muezzin calls the Adhan calling us all to pray.
The cousins are all in one room catching up with each other,
Our parents are spending time with their father and their mother.
Everyone is talking deep into the night,
The cousins pretend to be asleep when outside becomes light.
After shopping, the next day, the youngsters put on a fashion show,
The adults all comment on how everyone has grown.
The whole family go out in the evening to get ice cream,
We don't realise then, how much these moments will mean.
Now everyone's grown up and gone their own ways,
What we would do to go back to those summer holidays.

Trust in Him

When the floor crumbles underneath your feet
Darkness surrounds you making you doubt everything
Friends look more like enemies
And you don't recognise yourself in the mirror anymore
Loneliness seems inevitable and hope seems impossible
The night will end and day time will come
Trust in Him (SWT).